STRUGGLE FOR INTIMACY

STRUGGLE FOR INTIMACY

Kavya Sharma

Hawakal Publishers
New Delhi | Calcutta

HAWAKAL
New Delhi | Calcutta

HAWAKAL PUBLISHERS
70 B/9 Amritpuri, East of Kailash, New Delhi 65
33/1/2 K B Sarani, Mall Road, Calcutta 80

Email info@hawakal.com
Website www.hawakal.com

Cover photo: Shutterstock

Cover designed by Bitan Chakraborty

First edition (paperback) January 2022

ISBN: 978-93-91431-38-9 (paperback)

Price: INR 300 | USD 13.99

For
Amma,
now and forever

CONTENTS

OF LANGUAGES

OF LOCATIONS

OF FOOD AND SMELLS

PREFACE

Struggle for Intimacy began as a post-colonial thesis project for my Masters in Creative Writing at the University of Nottingham. Back in 2017, I had a collection of fifteen poems on themes surrounding ethnocentrism, racism, xenophobia, and the ever so controversial inter-racial love. Now, this book feels complete. These poems came out of my own experiences in a foreign country, from the colonial stories I heard from my grandmother and some out of imagination. My professors Jon Mcgregor, Leela, and Spencer Jordon, motivated me to continue writing the poems and work further on this project.

Some poems took a day to formalize, some years. With over four years on this book, I am finally ready to let this vulnerability out in the world. Dear reader, I hope this book finds its desired place somewhere near you.

Read. Breathe. Grasp.

Kavya Sharma
Jan 2022
New Delhi

OF LANGUAGE

YOUR LINGO, MINE

> "Friends and comrades, the light has gone out of our lives, and there is darkness everywhere, and I do not quite know what to tell you or how to say it. Our beloved leader, Bapu as we called him, The Father of the Nation, is no more."
>
> —Erstwhile Prime Minister
> Jawaharlal Nehru on Mahatma Gandhi

I have sustained within me a pitiful mix of jargons,
though born in an era post sick aftermaths,
they mingle within playfully shambling my sen—
tences from reflecting nation-pride and authority.

> Baba said it's a gift we didn't ask for and
> yet till today our soil smells of stomping
> boots and war; many died while the living breed to
> to tell stories of divided self and subdued
> minds. Do you recall?

I speak *jaise* you wouldn't ever,
my words rest in ambiguity in the
need to choose the ones that belong
to me and the ones to whom I belong.

> Who knows? *Kon jaane?*
> slow sipping nostalgia, he left out a breath

of unfinished memories on rewind, his
vision obscured by the fiery past our an—
cestors left behind dying cold-blooded.

Am I not a slave to your ing-lish even now?
it runs in our blood and passes on still, it will
till I begin to think of mine — crushed under
dusted papers, written by ancient poets.

My grandfather was a spy- *behroopia:*
wearing faces, he'd roam around crying free
dom, Baba said he marched with Bapu to
taste his own salt, to dip his own wounds in
the very waters where living meets the dead.

There is no cultural sentiment,
the emotion thrives on a shaky past and yet
I cling to your lingo, spilling — defining
my moment of knowledge, and yours?

History retorts at our comforts, the
one we all cage in our hearts, the one
we wouldn't speak of, the one you
wouldn't remember, while I struggle for
intimacy in your language.

LOVE, IN COLLOQUIAL ABUSES

i've kissed a man before
and felt the hurricane
destructing homes right
under my wayward tongue,
they taste of prolonged
bus-stand stares and pash's
poetry on abandoned
roof-tops
my city leapt fearless
into the stranger's arms,
this diabolic poem its
only witness—
his skin on mine felt like
aunt jennifer's chocolate
mud pie, his two weeks
old beard tickling my
insomnia to final death,
i can now dream about
him with my eyes open,
his history sustains his
ammi burning her post—
colonial desires behind
a netted burqa while
his abba manages to
murder azaadi into
perfectly shaped hukka
rings, bibi coughs her
usual—
his scent merging into

mine, i smell of my grand—
mother's rug that hasn't
been washed for over
two years now;
the memories of
nonno killing another
hindustani still intact—
who said love hasn't
been distorted in all
these human years,
my english now sounds
like his urdu's last rights,
here- they stain rivers
to disenable their sins;
the distance created
has to be mended with
lish's sealed behind
freedom
till another
white man approaches
my poetry with deceit
and we learn to call
ourselves lovers in
colloquial abuses;

tonight his kiss will
not taste poetic enough,
tonight his touch will fear
another war, tonight our
hurricanes will destroy
each other's cities;
tonight we'll
use our respective
mother tongues to
distort love a little
more.

INJURED TONGUE

it sticks to my tongue;
the dust that you spew through your accent,
the unsaid vowels rest unheard
I roll my tongue and you spit;
jittery words slip through my mind
while your sounds turn into whispers,
the last alphabets you often quaff
I miss your R's and O's
lord knows I try so hard to imitate your twang
yet it drools down my mouth
in an uncut version — twisted unalarmed
savage are your ways to alter my persistent drawl,
it lingers behind zonked.
I roll
un-roll
while you laugh at my injured tongue.

LINGUAL LOVE

She adjusted it, carefully holding her burgundy white hem, her colours, her pallu— the loose end of her sari— a garment wrapped around the body. Did you understand? She wore it for him, her aadmi— man, the one whose rang— colour was safed— white. Breathing beside the khidki-window, she adjusted her laal bindi— a red decorative mark worn in the middle of the forehead. South Asian Vanity. He liked it though, her conventional attires. He fancied her raw, untouched, devi— goddess like. She appeared alag- different to his native expectations. Oh! So pavitra— chaste, mulayam— soft, videshi— exotic. He heard her boli— speak and stunned smiled at her akarshan— charms. She had them ingrained for people she didn't belong to, she was nai— new. He came closer and she took a step back, sharam— shy. Did he understand? Her teachings were different, olden. He was fascinated, his need to go paas— near growing. He had to touch her bhoori tvacha— dusky skin, breathe it in, savour it, a newborn intrigue. She bit her hoonth— lips, craving the berang firang— colourless foreigner. Hawa chali— a gush of wind passed through them, making them embrace the other's ekta— oneness. Were they not ek now? Was this not lingual love?

VEGAN WOES

It was a stench of some sort, I swallowed my stagnant saliva stuck of stubborn swedging
bubbling within my bombastic bare open boat bazoo, bringing in faint belatedness
the one I threw thrashing towards the theatre artist, tasteless tiny tuna tethering
betwixt my mushy mouth mingling with miserly mango taste, last Monday
I remember relishing it with rotten Rogan Josh regretted rather recently.
I am an amateur vegan against the ambush antagonism of my ancestors,
half-wolf / half-human, hiding hither with unattended howling hushes,
father frowned saying: falguni you are far from being foreign
learning the lesson unlearned I languished in my language—
a mundane mix of matra bhasha and colonized mutuality
divided in roots, desperate distractions disregarded
calling for closure, jingoism cried crosschecking
withdrawal led to —where do I belong?
analysing the analogy of undone affinity
I knew new knowledge was unnerving
yet I yearned for practised eulogy
to trace my untrained traditions
and inherent identity
evolving elsewhere.

OF LOCATIONS

THE SUN HERE RISES FROM THE EAST

Every morning after five
I hear bells ringing in my ears,
the gods wake up only an hour before
while mother used to chastise her being,
taking hour long baths, chanting mantras
that'll bring them back to idols she
stubbornly prayed all her life,
cleaning dust and anger off their eyes
she'd place freshly plucked marigolds
grown in old silver teapots
under winter light,
the sun here rises from the east
where the men selling cow-milk
travel on cheaply bought bicycles,
two warning rings and you know
they've got what you feed to the almighty
milk rich in fat
no beggar's food
Aiii ...
she'd sing from behind the mesh windows,
running errands, ringing chimes
market bought incense sticks filling our noses;
a diya to guide her way into the heavens
where lived the one she lived for
and every day, today
while the city slept wrapped in
morning chill and hope
they were awake
i mean—
the feeder, the fed; and my Amma.

MY FRIEND HARIYA

while i was healing in the limpid
gullies of Dilli bazaar, i met Hariya,
he had two and a half broken teeth
but a heart that melted at the sound
of sweet slurps of roadside chuski,
and half-baked pani puris
and hot pakoras with mirchi,
the overly sweetened
bhudi k baal *(candy floss)*
was his favourite though—
so every morning
he'd rush holding his father's labour
hands to get hold of the finest,
most pinkish packets of the sweet that he sold
rolling his sleeves and tongue shouting
slogans of desperate attempts at people
who had instruments hanging down
their ears like pure sciences;
they all appeared like snake charmers
but Hariya with a token of his wide smile
and excellent enthusiasm
gathered a coin or two to purchase
the delicacy for himself:
his father thought he'd be a wonderful engineer,
he knew it too
a word of English and care
not me; listen, fast food, best

how could he let him sell for meager
coins but Hariya knew the art
of the treachery, almost ancestral—
he was the master of self,
of beautiful love and affection
oh! how funny
Each day after selling ten packets,
he'd gift the last one to himself saying:
Ayee Hariyaa ka baal le lo

RELIGIOUS HOME

i grew up in search of homes,
in rotting gullies under leaking skies
breathing cack smelling open gutters
of animal and human sewage alike.
mother said: *your home lies within you.*
so i set up on the task of building one
in every nook of my ill-defined existence.

they were cubbyholes of censored chants
and foreign invasions, of men with banners
and impressive hate poems, of acid attacks
and regenerating skin, of yomping second sex with
stripped deities, of biting teeth and unattended
graves, of gaping ruts and burning walls
of you and many I's.

9 MINUTES TO LAL BAGH

it's 9 minutes to
LAL BAGH
but the signal towards my left
is jam-packed and cluttered
I see women carrying little babies
sucking their dupattas with half-open
toothless little mouths and
un-affordable destinies—
the Hanuman idol stands
old and tired on my dashboard,
I see children below eight selling
Gods for ten rupees per idol
far-off
a man cleaning man-hole
stares back at the melting sun in disgust
what irony
i honk and honk till another
little girl cleans my window with
a dirty yellow cloth,
I see she holds a baby who wailed and wailed
till fed-up I gave ten rupees to human nourishment
but the gods cried in anger
I needed some
Milk
Honey and a
Fetish for a month to shake off the sins—
Tuesday's were usually spent saving money

off the temple donations—
towards my left is a boy selling balloons
I see he looks just fine;
a missing tooth on the front
and a grey REE-BOCK shirt
The REE on the right side is faded and dis-coloured
I stare at him till irritated he knocks on my window and
I pull down only to freeze for some expression
it's 9 minutes to Lal Bagh
and the signal is full of people
i choose to not know.

KAVI NIWAAS

A mile or two away from
jahangirpuri road,
towards your right and my left
was a little street of
distressed happy faces,
of old hobbies
and family businesses,
of uncles and aunts with
steady income and
bargained
stalls—
of little decorated shops
aside paan stained walls,
of scraped yellow paint and
quotes that say:
PEEING IN OPEN NOT ALLOWED

if you look a little carefully
you might find a shiny thing
or two in the garbage
bony street dogs smell all day
wagging their little tails
after their day tours to the nearby
Expensive flats, the back of which
faces this un-structured gully
of arts and crafts
of hand-made Taj-Mahals

and glass pen-cases
of wired chokers
and cheap lipsticks
of rings made of leftover trash
Of ten rupee kajal pencils
of shopkeepers we fight with
for a rupee or two less
of old people with grandchildren
frolicking around with
torn school bags
Dear reader,
If you manage to walk
through this lane of utter
misery and life
do visit me.

I sit cornered
in this very location
in an old house with barren garden
on a broken chair
my father left
before dying
The hammered board on the black gate reads:
"KAVI NIWAAS"

RESIDUE

and while half of me
is made of city dust,
the other half is of
leftover residue that
floats over ganga
nonchalant,
it doesn't shrug away
the past like we do.

FROM THE LAND OF CULTURES TO THE LAND OF GOD

It's an ancient city
A pilgrimage
but not for those who carry
the weight of their dead ones;
heavily beating heart
crying pain and relief-
there flows the woman;
The goddess
swifter than a dying soul
she doesn't sit, or rest
never remains but returns
fierce and dolorous
she carries within
her womanly parts
the remains of the deceased,
the sinner
the weak
the one who wouldn't return,
the one who unwinds within her arms—
A mother
A lover
The night
she helps them sleep
and travel to a world of
no infinity, no death
have you seen her?

floating around
Waiting...
to hold your hand
and take you along
from the land of cultures
to the land of god.

LONDON RAIL

It's cold and sunny
but the sky is clear blue
like my Scottish professor's eyes
the shade alters every time
I blink,
I see moving trains
jibber-jabber
the sounds turn into flying pigeons—
it's cold so i sniff under the shawl
mother made with her own warm hands,
it's red wool and
soft touches;
still smelling of her
sandalwood fingers
I am underground,
it stinks weird
I sneeze and breathe-
I miss a beat
saved!
but people pass by in a whim
jibber-jabber
flushed cheeks
it's cold.
shimla is colder
Amma would have said—
I shiver under her shawl
luke warm,

another train passes by—
I am empty log
frozen
jibber-jabber
7:35 a.m.
I am cold.

OF FOOD AND SMELLS

DUSSHERI

blow up
your air of expertise
let me gulp it like the
pulp of unripe mangoes
Bibi used to slice
without knives; on instinct,
carefully segregating
the green ones from the yellow
she'd hold it firm,
her legs in padmasana
then
cupping it within her hands,
she rotated it slowly
towards her right
and the world's left
again
-and-
again
with pressure on its skin
slowly coming off like changing seasons—
she'd smile at the sound of
her thursday market bangles,
the ones father got after
months of shy encounters;
bringing it close to her
thick lips painted red
guzzling the mush

she licked it childlike
from her shaggy upper lip
and said: *that's how you eat a dussehri*
(guarded)
I wiped it off
like a gentlewoman.

MASHED POTATOES WITH TOR-TI-AH

What can I get you?
Mashed potatoes with tor-ti-ah

Gulam Sahaab was open till late after;
poor old man, two years back I saw
him painting the chairs green in the
backyard of the Gulam Sons Café,
the sons ran south, crossing bridges
he couldn't run on without his
yearly painted garbage crutches.

What can I get you?
Mashed potatoes with tor-ti-ah

The empty chairs and tables were
quieter than the 3p.m. british night
Gulam Sahaab took a minute to walk
wobbly on his one and a half leg,
bending on his front desk he
checked the score, Ind vs Pak
and I stare back at my rival.

What can I get you?
Mashed potatoes with tor-ti-ah

Gulam Sahaab wets his index finger
counting his daily income, converting

them to rupees he'd never get back,
he licks his finger— twice thrice
reminding me of father searching
for hundreds among the biggies
for my school picnics to Milk Factory.

What can I get you?
Mashed potatoes with tor-ti-ah

I notice him wearing a burgundy kurta
with white pyjama stitched with octagon
embroidery, it's Eid al-Fitr and I smell
home from behind his counters,
Gulam Sahaab waits for the night
while it's 10 p.m. in the land where
the sun and the moon are the oppressors.

What can I get you again?
Maashed potaato with Tor-tilla

I fumble with no diction while
Gulam Sahaab *as-salaam-alaikum's*
me with his wrinkled smile giving me
a bowl full of sheer khurma stirred with
crushed almonds and saffron delight.
Eid Mubarak! He says
In his forsaken Urdu stresses.

CASHMERE CHAI

We were little then, little enough for our mouths to be stuffed with cerelac every few hours. Hungry enough for more though. Salivating through our baby pink insides on hardly developed funny chins. Mother got us little motorbikes with red lights and cars with strong gears, cards with bulky men and a few largely breasted women, plastic cricket bats with plastic balls and squeaky moneys and dogs and bears and elephants and humans and what not. While Dad came home from his rendezvous with smiles and travel stories. Once upon a time he'd say and I was there already, exactly where he wanted us to be. He'd sit on the dusted white netted swing hung from the ceiling in the balcony with no air but fragrance of a far-off land-Of gunpowder and other ingredients of divided jingoism. Little curls of fog coalescing with the dry sky, white cup with red blue flowers tiltedly printed, rare beauty of my father's select and we were amazed. We got milk in steel glasses with family name imprinted on its un-cornered roundabout. Coiling up in the porcelain cup it left behind on the insides its pure mist and sweet floral scoosh. Sexed up with a table spoon or two of mildly crushed fennel seeds, cardamom and a few lightly toasted almonds. Honey gold, it smelled of cashew nuts and traditional spices. Sluuurr-rrppppp he'd take it in and Ahhhhh he'd breathe out his very own elite expensively bought Cashmere chai.

OF APPEARANCE

MIYA

colour me yellow Miya
for I am mud wrapped
in shiny sarees,
they see me changing
shapes
now and then
I carry off-beat realities
in my bland wrists
and swollen eyes—

some days I am red
smeared in areas you touch
with your eyes closed;
I am farther Miya—
from the milk shop that
sells toned milk
and bra shops with white faces,
from sleeveless lives
and dresses that make
me look city clean—

Miya, I am dust laid on old
sandooks and stone floors,
I am Marilyn Monroe under
cotton quilts,
I am, the bird dipped in charcoal,
it's time you see I have no horns,

no nails to get myself a pair
of something you own with women
who like their tea dark—

it's windows and creepers
I peep through to get past
a reality you and they
chose for me,
my bangles Miya,
they ring in regret;
i am uptight and personal
when you seek romance behind kitchen corridors,
Amma would have looked me in the eye
and said *don't.*

Do you see what fate
I hold in my lined hands?
I wallow in eternity you
provide me with your
labour hands
and sexist undertones,
Miya, for I carry within
what you and I
suffer in silence.

MIXED RACE

Chad said my hair looked like Bob Marley's
but I sounded like a dying Sufi poet,
that my voice is coarse and pitch black
and he feels the need to clear his throat
before he can listen to me;
that during dawn I smelled of curry
but hey! I look like a girl who can
gulp a can or two of rot-gut;
A girl...
a girl who can fling a few men
and go to temple for evening prayers
he said I had belly fat, but I could
pull off an off-shoulder dragon tattoo
that I could skip college but get
beaten up by my father for indecency,
he said I had eyes stretched out to limits
no man could reach without dying
but my thicker lips were enough to
call for unwanted attention,
he said my pits were darker than
the rest of my skin but that didn't
make me a mixed race,
that my nose ring was more
far-flung than the one on my navel,
he said unlike girls he had seen I
seduced him with kohl under my eyes,
that nylon colours would suit my skin

under no moonshine
that I am a silent sleeper, but I laugh
louder than my gut allows me to,
the kind who could pull of a
bikini but not sun burns
he said I wasn't traditional the way
he saw in movies,
that he wouldn't date a girl like
me but he often dreamt of one
that seemed distantly familiar.

MEN ON MY SIDE OF THE WORLD

It begins for a woman
with the first two buds
on her chest;
once leveled
left untouched
in patience we wait
for men with open legs and arms
from behind the peepal tree,
across the roads and
moving cars,
along flowing rivers
and steep mountains
appear thirsty eyes
that feel us with the touch of the wind
travelling scents of un-expressed emotions
in sturdy hearts and
beating desires
coveting
but mannered we look away
I look away too
locking the cave to our hearts,
(in the name of doctored traditions)
it takes us time to give in,
in this art of eternal treachery;
I steal a glimpse and stare at
the ceiling all night long
while the stars shine on my face

reminding me of men I turned away from
as a ritual in my delicate lode
Amma calls me
for the one sitting in my veranda
the koyal finally coo's
while he sips cold roohafza
in his grey tailored suit
and polished shoes
<Slurrpp>
His lips flat unlike our village roads
indistinct voices
I stare down till I shed seeing
a blurry vision of myself in his
shiny shoes—
I hear laughs
of my confirmation
Oh! (But I am yet to look)
Rajni Bua indicates her disapproval
pressing my hand hard
Once twice—

on my side of the world
we make our men wait.

STINKING OF NERUDA POEMS

I've known a woman
who isn't soft
she has thorns
all over her cradle skin,
it's warm
when you go near
she stinks of leapt over memories
and Neruda poems,
I see her tearing pages every day
scratching the words
that stick by nonetheless,
she paints them black
with her bare fingers
and silent soul
I have seen her parching her lips
for some more hate through
unknown men on shady side-walks,
I've known her drunk on
monday mornings—
I've seen her grow lust
in her milked bosom,
I've seen her smeared in
her own blood,
she walks hand-in-hand
with blinding winds
I've seen her screaming into
their foreboding

rejecting known symbols,
I've known her fierce;
she sustains her own winter,
it rests within her sea-green veins and callous whispers
the white fog of tainted wisdom—
I've known a woman
who isn't soft
and I've kissed her
now and then.

MEAT MARKET

I am misery
wrapped in vermillion
they sell at the meat market
near Devi-temple
today and tomorrow
i'll be reminded
that I belong.

LIVING DEAD

She always lay on the corner towards the side-wall of our room, her back, round and curved. The wall was the kind of blue that'd drown you to sadness- somewhere between navy blue and sea blue, a cough or two and I knew she lived to witness a generation of unavoidable ignorance. Her saree tucked high above in unmatched petticoat,

one over the other—

Brown legs, they were lined, as if she walked... she walked for years to keep us safe. All over her hands I felt a kind of roughness that makes one dead inside and yet when she saw me, I saw her smiling at my unwillingness to exist. Seconds into the moment and I was teary.

Was I teary of the present she longed to be in?

Every day, I counted not the time but the breaths she lost talking about the past that was.

"We were farmers. Pitaji walked on foot for 22 kilometers to get fresh seeds. English took everything away."

She knew a word or two of English
Upper Caste
Farmers
Rich
English/England
Simon
I laughed, now and then I cried too.
Tick-tock
A cough or two, she was alive.

COCONUT OIL AND GUTTER WATER

Slender arms
I see veins spread
like spider-webs,
butter waists
and eyes that seal a
fragile tomorrow—
surrender:
at the count of
three
two
one...
let lose
to men who come around
for renewal; from happy sad wives
some complain of hairy pits
others
of hair that smell of
coconut oil and gutter water—
unfed little bodies
and their shimmery clothes,
hanging lose
like crow-wings
a fuchsia lipstick they all share
their fate smeared in nympholepsy—
a clap and they all swirl
like a puppet without strings.

A Juliet's balcony
containing their breasts
and whistles;
at the end of the gully
is a police man who sells death wishes
and a woman dies cheap.

OF SUPERSTITION AND OTHER EVILS

DEAD BABIES INSIDE MY WOMB

Mother, last night when you found just
the right man for me,
i felt my colours merging between my legs,
a warm welcome—
i waited at the doorstep while
you decided my price split into
three and half installments of
crossing the borders at the risk
of being shot or worse,
returned untouched;
my flesh curls into circles of destiny
that lie accustomed to where i leave
my buttons loose, i walk and walks with me
my hanging bottom;
a dog or two stares back in disgust
and i frown at my possibility of being
just a pair of heavy bosom
and bulked corners,
the homes around feel suffocating:
it's tired hands and city sins,
i quietly prayed the Satan that dawn and
validated my existence down the
the huge tree and thick rains,
better than any brown man with his bare hands could,
i unhooked till there wasn't enough revoking left,
my fingers smelt of ginger on uncut onions but i
rang my temple bells vigorous and repetitive

without cleaning the shrines;
oh how do i gift birth to another me,
when i still needed a man who'd
come home drunk every other day
only to sow dead babies inside my womb.

BLACK CAT

It's a slow walk to the grocery store,
I need
two shampoos
a sandalwood stick
and a matchbox.
I am bad at math
but baba said it'll cost us
rupees fifty-seven,
he gave me Rupees sixty
I need three back—
three back
that's easy math.

It's a slow walk to the grocery store
but I need a black cat
to die of superstition;
one that cleverly
crosses my way
before I see...
it's bad luck and death
but I've been saved before
pushed ahead
pulled back—
it favors me more,
I mean
the black cat.

FIND ME

(In the name of Religion)

Find me in denoted temples
full of blood-smeared foreheads,
find me now in your lined palms,
find me dear devotee
in your dazed whisper
find me tainted in your scars—

Read them out loud to me,
the things that you write
in my name—
find me in earthen scriptures
torn apart
find me crooning under your
heavy heart
find me in between a million
death wishes and lost lives
find me now and then
flaming amidst ancestral pyre—

Find me breathless in milk and honey,
find me dead under lost wishes
but when eyes closed you bow down
to idols that dress and speak like you
find me dear in a meager setting
within you—
you don't go around crying freedom

in a world full of broken homes
there are humans living on steroids;
it's a lazy road to extinction
but we manage blues
under our oceans—

steel glasses full of
luke warm milk
dirty pants hanging
on a cornered chair
unfolded quilts
cracked windows
plates full of leftover ghee
thin brown hands;
Amma merges emotions with hunger—

the manholes stinks of
tired working-class hands;
I see walking legs minding steps
the roads to location are tattered
like our existence
but I live nearer to a
bookish reality—

with a voice that breaks every
hour into pieces of love and hope
Amma begs for a little dream every morning,
the idols are orange
And white
And shades of blue
but they all smile back
like they belong to you
How many steps ahead are you
from your own failure?

You don't take dips in waters full of floating bodies
and leftovers of a monotonous monstrosity
you don't sit with your legs folded
you don't throw your face in your palms,
you don't look out of that window;
you don't see life
You don't surrender to one rupee coins
you don't sit across
crying freedom
in world
where every hour
Amma breaks her silence
sharing love and existence.

OF WARS (AND HOMES)

SISTERHOOD OF RAGING NATIONS

When I met her, I knew the blood that travelled in our veins was from ancestors that spent a lifetime of togetherness, she wasn't different, nothing alien about the groundedness in her voice, a lingering for a home where doors were wide open for people to come in and rest in caring arms. My home was no contrary, the very caring arms that lulled people into love, took up guns and fire to bomb each other's devotion, to destroy families that carried the same soil, to fail nations that endured grieving hearts.

When I met her, I was aware of the hate that she carried- it wasn't conflicting to mine. How the moment we were born we were told we are separate from people that lived on the same land (once) — together we cursed an era of slaughter yet quietly within our singing hearts. The silence that ensued was similar to the one we experienced when they taught us P.A.R.T.I.T.I.O.N written bold and beautiful. How could we run away now when years back we ran away from each other?

When I met her, I knew we were same- with homogenous intentions of poisoning our antidotes flushing our cheeks with anger and histories with authenticities; we shared a night they left behind for us to decide our fate under no stars… a language they bestowed before snatching away souvenirs we never gifted (our pride wrapped in shiny papers) while we mounted onto it for the elite to present our poorly structured emotions. We carry the same pride today; only, it shines within us against the foe, once a friend.

When I met her, I knew we were once the oppressed and together we languished in a state of rotten self and power hunger, so much so that we- ready to kill and survive damned our own unity and loss to gain over each other a power that belonged to none. We closed our eyes for the fire to take us in, live and moving, losing little of what existed and perishing altogether the ties we never decided on. Now, when I see you, I know you are the enemy I'd fight with for the one that created a yesterday we never wished for.

When I see you, I know we share a sisterhood of raging nations.

DEAR OCCIDENT

Dear Occident,
in my attempt to define
my meaning in your exposition
I lost a few thousand sages
praying under Banyan trees,
they sat naked
in dhayaana
when you blew magic
from the other side of the world.

Dear Occident,
in my need to prove my merit
I disassociated the existence of human race
from any four-legged wild,
but while I communicated
wallowing my tongue
all the way back
I felt
I started a whole new civilization.

Dear Occident,
while I was trying to find
reasons that help us co-exist
you drew lines of danger—
for my habitat lacked
the lustre of growing pillars
and moving trains;

but sometimes I prefer
walking desert feet.

Dear Occident,
my spirituality reeks from within
a series of religions
with mortals and immortals
walking hand in hand
and while I bow down
to touch my elder's feet
I dive in river goddesses to shake off
the sins you gently rubbed on me.

Dear Occident,
every night before sleeping
I read the Chalisa—
it's a stotram dedicated
to the one, half of which many think
presents my entire race,
son of the wind god
he has a tail
and the face of a vanara.

Dear Occident,
every time my land shines
of blinding yellow
I go discoloured and dusty;
woodworm beetle
matt-brown
I bloom in the warmth
of my fervid climate.

Dear Occident,
when young
my mother took me

to the nearby temple
where a pandit
wearing saffron
read shlokas in Sanskrit,
he read my hand too
and said—
In future, I was to travel west.

Dear Occident,
you pronounce my name wrong
but it means poetry
काव्या
the syllables go
upside down
you don't just say it,
you sing it.
I welcome you home...

BECAUSE WE ARE A GENERATION FULL OF SECOND HAND SINS

While we were fighting our battles
on a land full of un-soaked blood
you gave in
at the sound of a bullet,
a distant scream of lost comrade
I fear politics is not one of your
major concerns:
back then
it was men wearing wet promises
on slippery tongues and
foreign accent;
trying to imitate god
in white skin and black suits,
diversity was brought in
by an unsaid pact in the language
you speak and I write in,
there was you and me
and beating chests but modernity
was the agenda we were looking for
in a country full of farmers and
language professors:
I WANT FREEDOM
I cried and you cried too
with a mouth full of
bitter-sweet history and

colonist agenda
do you recall being in the nation
you belonged to, only; it belonged
to someone else
for years when they waged war on people
with dubious identity and
funny dialects
what section do you belong to Sir?
the one that breaths the air of
In-dependent forgiveness or the one
that still grieves the loss of a million martyrs.
can you name one you did not
read in the local newspaper?
it was what they tell you about
people burning in hell
and walking naked feet on
the soil that once belonged;
for we are generation full of
forlorn conscience and
second-hand sins.